CONNECT BIBLE STUDIES

The Da Vinci Code

Dan Brown
(Corgi, 2003)

Secret knowledge
Symbolism
Religious authorities
Authentic faith

www.connectbiblestudies.com

connect
linking the Word to the world

CONNECT BIBLE STUDIES: *The Da Vinci Code*

Published by Scripture Union, 207–209 Queensway, Bletchley, MK2 2EB, England.
Scripture Union is an international Christian charity working with churches in more than 130 countries providing resources to bring the good news about Jesus Christ to children, young people and families – and to encourage them to develop spiritually through the Bible and prayer. As well as a network of volunteers, staff and associates who run holidays, church-based events and school Christian groups, Scripture Union produces a wide range of publications and supports those who use the resources through training programmes.
Email: info@scriptureunion.org.uk
Internet: www.scriptureunion.org.uk

British Library Cataloguing-in-Publication Data: a catalogue record for this book is available from the British Library.
First published 2005 ISBN 1 84427 160 9

ALSO AVAILABLE AS AN ELECTRONIC DOWNLOAD: www.connectbiblestudies.com

Cover design by Aricot Vert of Fleet, UK.

Printed and bound in the UK by Henry Ling, Dorchester.

Other titles in this series:

Harry Potter 1 85999 578 0	**TV Game Shows** 1 85999 609 4
Destiny's Child: *Survivor* 1 85999 613 2	**Lord of the Rings** 1 85999 634 5
The Simpsons 1 85999 529 2	**Dido: *No Angel*** 1 85999 679 5
Sven: *On Football* 1 85999 690 6	**Pullman: *His Dark Materials*** 1 85999 714 7
Friends 1 85999 775 9	**Madonna** 1 84427 032 7
James Bond 1 84427 007 6	**John Grisham's Thrillers** 1 84427 021 1
The Matrix Trilogy 1 84427 061 0	**TV Soaps** 1 84427 087 4
Computer Animated Films 1 84427 115 3	**The Star Wars Trilogy** 1 84427 147 1

Titles available as electronic download only:
U2: *All That You Can't Leave Behind*/ Billy Elliot/ Chocolat/ How to be Good/ AI: Artificial Intelligence/ Iris/ Superheroes
And more titles following. Check www.connectbiblestudies.com for latest titles or ask at any good Christian bookshop.

www.connectbiblestudies.com

connect

linking the Word to the world

Using Connect Bible Studies

What Are These Studies?

These innovative small group Bible studies have two aims. Firstly, to enable group members to dig into their Bibles and get to know them better. Secondly, by being based on contemporary films, books, TV programmes, music etc, the aim is to help people think through topical issues in a biblical way.

It is not envisaged that all members will always be able to watch the films, play the music or read the books, or indeed that they will always want to. A summary is always provided. However, our vision is that knowing about these films and books empowers Christians to engage with friends and colleagues about them. Addressing issues from a biblical perspective gives Christians confidence that they know what they think, and can bring a distinctive angle to bear in conversations.

The studies are produced in sets of four – ie four weeks' worth of group Bible Study material. These are available in print published by Scripture Union from your local Christian bookshop, or via the Internet at www.connectbiblestudies.com.

How Do I Use Them?

These studies are designed to stimulate creative thought and discussion within a biblical context. Each section therefore has a range of questions or options from which you as leader may choose in order to tailor the study to your group's needs and desires. Different approaches may appeal at different times, so the studies aim to supply lots of choice. Whilst adhering to the main aim of corporate Bible study, some types of questions may enable this for your group better than others – so take your pick.

Group members should be supplied with the appropriate sheet that they can fill in, each one also showing the relevant summary.

Leader's notes contain:

1 Opening questions

These help your group settle in to discussion, while introducing the topics. They may be straightforward, personal or creative, but aim to provoke a response.

2 Summary

We suggest the summary of the book or film will follow now, read aloud if necessary. There may well be reactions that group members want to express even before getting on to the week's issue.

3 Key issue

Again, either read from the leader's notes, or summarise.

4 Chapters to read

We've split the book into four chunks, for those groups who want to read a section of the book before each meeting.

5 Bible study

Lots of choice here. Choose as appropriate to suit your group – get digging into the Bible. Background reading and texts for further help and study are suggested, but please use the material provided to inspire your group to explore their Bibles as much as possible. A concordance might be a handy standby for looking things up. A commentary could be useful too, such as the *New Bible Commentary 21st Century Edition* (IVP, 1994). The idea is to help people to engage with the truth of God's word, wrestling with it if necessary, but making it their own.

Don't plan to work through every question here. Within each section the two questions explore roughly the same ground but from different angles or in different ways. Our advice is to take one question from each section. The questions are open-ended so each ought to yield good discussion – though of course any discussion in a Bible study may need prompting to go a little further.

5 Implications

Here the aim is to tie together the perspectives gained through Bible study and the impact of the book or film. The implications may be personal, a change in worldview, or new ideas for relating to non-churchgoers. Choose questions that adapt to the flow of the discussion.

6 Prayer

Leave time for it! We suggest a time of open prayer, or praying in pairs if the group would prefer. Encourage your members to focus on issues from your study that had a particular impact on them. Try different approaches to prayer – light a candle, say a prayer each, write prayers down, play quiet worship music – aiming to facilitate everyone to relate to God.

Further Reading

The Da Vinci Code has caused a stir in the Christian world, due to its allegations about Jesus and Mary Magdalene. If you would like to do some further reading into the book's theories, recommended books include *The Gospel Code* by Ben Witherington III (InterVarsity Press, 2004) and *The Rough Guide to the Da Vinci Code* (Rough Guides, 2004).

www.connectbiblestudies.com

connect

linking the Word to the world

The Da Vinci Code

Dan Brown (Corgi, 2003)

Part 1: Secret knowledge

'Everyone loves a conspiracy.'
(p232)

Please read Using Connect Bible Studies *(page 3) before leading a Bible study with this material.*

Opening Questions

Choose one of these questions.

Do you think some Christians are overreacting by condemning *The Da Vinci Code*? Why/why not?	What did you like/not like about *The Da Vinci Code*?
Why do you think *The Da Vinci Code* has sold so well?	Why are secrets attractive?

Summary

The Da Vinci Code opens as Jacques Saunière, curator of the Louvre art gallery in Paris, is shot and staggers to his death inside its Grand Gallery. Coded writing surrounds his spread-eagled body, so Captain Bezu Fache of the French Judicial Police calls in Robert Langdon, a visiting American professor of religious symbology, apparently to help decipher the code. However, Fache actually suspects Robert of the murder, because he was named by the coded writing. A French cryptologist, Sophie Neveu, arrives to assist. She convinces Robert that his life is in danger too, and escapes from custody with him. They want time to decode the message that Saunière has left, and to find that time, they need to go on the run.

Meanwhile, an albino monk named Silas is doing painful penance for having committed the murder. He is a member of Opus Dei, an organisation within Roman Catholicism which is facing expulsion by the Pope. Its leading Bishop, Manuel Aringarosa, Silas' mentor, has been persuaded by the enigmatically-named Teacher that documents exist which will give Opus Dei the power it needs to secure its place in the Catholic church. The documents have been guarded for centuries by a secret society, the Priory of Sion, of which Saunière was leader. They concern vital information the Catholic Church has suppressed.

The race is on for Robert and Sophie, desperately decoding Saunière's dying message before the police catch them, and for Silas, obeying the Teacher's commands. All are looking for the mysterious keystone, which will lead them to the secret Saunière died for. Sophie confesses she is Saunière's estranged granddaughter – she knows the code is for her to solve.

Key Issue: Secret knowledge

The Da Vinci Code, published in April 2003, has sold over ten million copies worldwide, and has been translated into many languages. Tom Hanks is starring in a Hollywood blockbuster adaptation, and it has turned its author, Dan Brown, into a multi-millionaire. Why is it so popular? Surely one reason is the way Dan Brown draws us in to his novel with multi-layered secrets about huge issues. Why was Saunière killed? What was his message to his granddaughter? What is Opus Dei really up to? What is the Catholic Church afraid of? What is the truth that only a few know? The secrets keep us turning the pages. So our study begins with some more questions. Is God a God of secrets, only revealing the truth to a few? Is there hidden 'truth' about to be told – and is it true anyway? Why are we so fascinated by secrets?

Chapters to read:
Read chapters 1 to 26.

Bible Study

Choose one question from each section.

1   Hesitation

> **Sophie stamped her foot. 'I told you I don't like secrets!'**
> **'Princess,' he smiled. 'Life is filled with secrets. You can't learn them all at once.'**
> (Sophie as a child and her grandfather, p142)

◆   Read Jeremiah 23:13–32. Why is God 'against the prophets' (v 30)? What should the prophets have recognised? How could they understand God's secret thoughts?

◆   Read Ephesians 3:1–13. Describe the secret that Paul is excited about. What is its purpose and effect?

2   God reveals secrets

> *'Whatever it is, my grandfather obviously wanted very badly to keep it secret.'*
> (Sophie, p274)

◆   Read Daniel 2:1–49. What aspects of God's character was Daniel grateful for? How was King Nebuchadnezzar affected?

◆   Read 1 Corinthians 2:1–16. What has God done with his major secrets? How can we know God's secrets?

3   The worst-kept secret

> *Sophie looked sceptical. 'My friends who are devout Christians definitely believe that Christ literally walked on water, literally turned water into wine and was born of a literal virgin birth.'* (p452)

◆   Read John 14:1–14. What do Philip and Thomas not understand? What does Jesus' relationship to the Father mean for us?

◆   Read Colossians 1:15–27. Who is Jesus? How does his identity affect us?

4   Secrets – true or false?

> *'Many Grail historians,' Teabing added, 'believe that if the Priory is indeed planning to release this truth, this point in history would be a symbolically apt time.'* (p358)

◆   Read 2 Timothy 3:10 – 4:5. How do we avoid myths? How do we know the truth?

◆   Read I John 2:18–27; 4:1–6. How do you know the difference between lies and truth? What are the implications of knowing the truth?

Leaders: 'we' in 1 John 4:6 refers to the apostles (see 1:1–4). Their witness supplements the emphasis on the Spirit's anointing in 2:20–27.

Implications

Many have made a trade of delusions and false miracles, deceiving the stupid multitude. – LEONARDO DA VINCI (p312)

Choose one or more of the following questions.

- ◆ Is *The Da Vinci Code* a genuine threat to Christianity/Christians? Why/why not?

- ◆ Does God feel near to you or far away at the moment? How can you either celebrate the former, or improve the latter?

- ◆ Are there aspects of Christianity, or the Bible, which actually do feel like they are veiled in secrecy? How could your group help with this? Is there other research you could do?

- ◆ Do you believe that God wants us to get to know him? In what ways are you following up this invitation?

- ◆ How confident are you that the New Testament and God are reliable – and that the real truth is not hidden away somewhere?

- ◆ What 'myths' about Jesus do you come up against in conversation with others? How do you respond, and how does it affect you? Are there ways to explain your own faith more effectively?

- ◆ Is there research you need to do to check out some of Dan Brown's theories – for your own sake or the sake of others who may ask you questions?

Prayer

Spend some time praying through these issues.

Members' Sheet – *The Da Vinci Code* Part 1

Summary

The Da Vinci Code opens as Jacques Saunière, curator of the Louvre art gallery in Paris, staggers to his death inside its Grand Gallery. Coded writing surrounds his spread-eagled body, so Captain Bezu Fache of the French Judicial Police calls in Robert Langdon, a visiting American professor of religious symbology, apparently to help decipher the code. However, Fache actually suspects Robert of the murder, because he was named by the coded writing. A French cryptologist, Sophie Neveu, arrives to assist. She convinces him that his life is in danger too, and escapes with him from the Louvre. They want time to decode the message that Saunière has left, and to find that time, they need to go on the run.

Meanwhile, an albino monk named Silas is doing painful penance for having committed the murder. He is a member of Opus Dei, an organisation within Roman Catholicism which is facing expulsion by the Pope. Its leading Bishop Manuel Aringarosa, Silas' mentor, has been persuaded by the enigmatically-named Teacher that documents exist which will give Opus Dei the power it needs to secure its place in the Catholic church. The documents have been guarded for centuries by a secret society, the Priory of Sion, of which Saunière was leader. They concern vital information the Catholic Church has suppressed.

The race is on for Robert and Sophie, desperately decoding Saunière's dying message before the police catch them, and for Silas, obeying the Teacher's commands. All are looking for the mysterious keystone, which will lead them to the secret Saunière died for. Sophie confesses she is Saunière's estranged granddaughter – she knows the code is for her to solve.

Key Issue

Bible Study notes

Implications

Prayer

The Da Vinci Code

Dan Brown (Corgi, 2003)

Part 2: Symbolism

'We are beginning to sense the need to restore the sacred feminine.'
(Marie Chauvel, p581)

Please read Using Connect Bible Studies *(page 3) before leading a Bible study with this material.*

Opening Questions

Choose one of these questions.

Do you find spiritual symbols helpful? Why/why not?	Do you think of God as being male? Why/why not?
In what way can symbols be powerful?	Were there symbols in *The Da Vinci Code* which surprised you? Why?

Summary

'13-3-2-21-1-1-8-5 O Draconian devil! O Lame Saint! PS. Find Robert Langdon'

The murdered Saunière's code leads Robert and Sophie to Da Vinci's *Madonna on the Rocks*. The fleur-de-lis on the key behind this painting, together with the Da Vinci links, lead Robert to conclude that Saunière is connected with the Priory of Sion. The two fugitives, suspected of murder by the police, take refuge at the house of eccentric British knight, Sir Leigh Teabing, who is a friend of Robert's. Teabing introduces Sophie to the notion that the Holy Grail is not a cup but is a woman – Mary Magdalene. Teabing suggests that it is actually Mary Magdalene sitting to the right of Jesus in Da Vinci's painting of *The Last Supper*, and that Jesus really entrusted his church to her, not to the disciple Peter, as Gnostic gospels elucidate. She is symbolic of the sacred feminine, the Rose line, which has been suppressed by the church for centuries, and needs to be restored. The two overlaid triangles of the Star of David, the signs for male and female – the blade and the chalice – are all symbols which point to the pagan equality of god and goddess. Hints to this truth can be found in art and history, especially in the works of Leonardo Da Vinci. In fact, Sophie's grandfather was estranged from her because she witnessed his involvement in a ritual sexual act, whereby the male experiences the divine in union with the female. Harmony in society will come with the union of male and female divine in us all.

The church has misled the world. Only a privileged few know the truth about Jesus Christ – that he was married to Mary Magdalene and had a daughter; that these two women escaped to France and their descendants still live; that the Holy Grail refers also to Jesus' bloodline. Teabing joins the race to find the vital keystone. A cryptex – an encoded hollow cylinder – which is in the safe deposit box opened by the key leads them all to London and more codes and secrets.

Key Issue: Symbolism

Dan Brown's twisting plot takes us on a breathtaking race from one mysterious symbol to the next, intertwined with codes and explanations galore. Nothing is sacred as far as the plot is concerned, and Brown reels in mathematical, Christian, religious and pagan symbols, mixing them with art and history… While some judicious digging might reveal Brown as cavalier in his interpretations, our purpose here is to set some of his suggestions against biblical material. What does the Bible say about the significance of Mary Magdalene? How does it define God? Is sex really a way to experience God? Does the Bible see symbols as a trail of difficult codes leading to the truth?

Chapters to read:

Read chapters 27 to 53.

Bible Study

Choose one question from each section.

1   Mary Magdalene – symbol of?

> *… the Rose was a symbol that spoke of the Grail on many levels – secrecy, womanhood and guidance – the feminine chalice and guiding star that lead to secret truth.* (p275)

◆   Read Luke 8:1–3; John 19:25; John 20:1–18. How would you describe Mary Magdalene's relationship with Jesus from this evidence? What is the significance of the events in John 20:1–18?

> *Leaders: see 1 Corinthians 9:5. Surely Paul would have mentioned Jesus' wife to bolster his argument here, if Jesus had been married. Also, Isaiah 53:10–12 suggests that the Messiah's descendants would be spiritual rather than mortal.*

◆ Read John 13:1–17; Luke 22:14–23. What did Jesus want his disciples to learn? Compare the symbols of water, bread and blood.

Leaders: Leonardo Da Vinci's The Last Supper *is reputedly based on John's account.*

2 God – symbol of male and female deities?

> *The Star of David ... the perfect union of male and female ... Solomon's Seal ... marking the Holy of Holies, where the male and female deities – Yahweh and Shekinah – were thought to dwell.* (Robert's thoughts, p584)

◆ Read Genesis 1:27; Matthew 23:37–39. What can we learn about the nature of God from these passages? How does symbolism help our understanding?

◆ Read Isaiah 49:13–18; Hosea 11:1–4. What can we learn about the nature of God from these passages? How does symbolism help our understanding?

3 Sex – symbol of divine experience?

> *'Intercourse was the revered union of the two halves of the human spirit – male and female – through which the male could find spiritual wholeness and communion with God. What you saw was not about sex, it was about spirituality.' (Teabing, p411)*

◆ Read Song of Songs 7:1 – 8:4. What is the aim of all that the lovers appreciate about each other, and how do they express this?

◆ Read Ephesians 5:25–33. What does Paul see as the significance of 'two become one' – for a married couple and for the church?

4 Symbols – secret codes?

> *Each block was carved with a symbol, seemingly at random, creating a cipher of unfathomable proportion ... To this day the Rosslyn Trust offered a generous reward to anyone who could unveil the secret meaning, but the code remained a mystery.* (p570)

◆ Read Exodus 12:1–15; 1 Corinthians 5:6–8. What did the lamb symbolise for the Hebrews? How does Paul develop this idea in his words to the Corinthians?

◆ Read John 6:25–59. In what ways does Jesus share insights into his identity with his listeners? Where does symbolism end and straight talking begin in Jesus' words?

Implications

'I serve a far greater master than my own pride. The Truth. Mankind deserves to know that truth. The Grail found us all, and now she is begging to be revealed.'
(Teabing, p537)

Choose one or more of the following questions.

◆ What is the role and importance of symbols in the Christian faith?

◆ What relevance does Mary Magdalene have to the good news of the Gospels?

◆ How would you answer someone who accuses the church of historically suppressing the role of women?

◆ What is the attraction of fertility-based goddess worship, or the idea of dual male and female deities?

◆ It has been suggested that understanding and worshipping God as 'parent' might be more helpful than 'father'. What is your response to this?

◆ Do you think Dan Brown brings an authentic challenge to a male-dominated society regarding how women are viewed and treated? Why/why not?

◆ What is sex for? How does this compare to the way sex is used in *The Da Vinci Code*?

◆ What does Jesus' treatment of women say about the way he viewed them?

◆ If we are made in the image of God, as male and female, what would you say about *The Da Vinci Code*'s understanding of male-plus-female-equals-divine?

Prayer

Spend some time praying through these issues.

Members' Sheet – *The Da Vinci Code* Part 2

Summary

'13-3-2-21-1-1-8-5 O Draconian devil! O Lame Saint! PS. Find Robert Langdon'

The murdered Saunière's code leads Robert and Sophie to Da Vinci's *Madonna on the Rocks*. The fleur-de-lis on the key behind this painting, together with the Da Vinci links, lead Robert to conclude that Saunière is connected with the Priory of Sion. The two fugitives, suspected of murder by the police, take refuge at the house of eccentric British knight, Sir Leigh Teabing, who is a friend of Robert's. Teabing introduces Sophie to the notion that the Holy Grail is not a cup but is a woman – Mary Magdalene. Teabing suggests that it is actually Mary Magdalene sitting to the right of Jesus in Da Vinci's painting of *The Last Supper*, and that Jesus really entrusted his church to her, not to the disciple Peter, as Gnostic gospels elucidate. She is symbolic of the sacred feminine, the Rose line, which has been suppressed by the church for centuries, and needs to be restored. The two overlaid triangles of the Star of David, the signs for male and female – the blade and the chalice – are all symbols which point to the pagan equality of god and goddess. Hints to this truth can be found in art and history, especially in the works of Leonardo Da Vinci. In fact, Sophie's grandfather was estranged from her because she witnessed his involvement in a ritual sexual act, whereby the male experiences the divine in union with the female. Harmony in society will come with the union of male and female divine in us all.

The church has misled the world. Only a privileged few know the truth about Jesus Christ – that he was married to Mary Magdalene and had a daughter; that these two women escaped to France and their descendants still live; that the Holy Grail refers also to Jesus' bloodline.

Teabing joins the race to find the vital keystone. A cryptex – an encoded hollow cylinder – which is in the safe deposit box opened by the key leads them all to London and more codes and secrets.

Key Issue

Bible Study notes

Implications

Prayer

www.connectbiblestudies.com

connect
linking the Word to the world

The Da Vinci Code

Dan Brown (Corgi, 2003)

Part 3: Religious authorities

'... history is always written by the winners.'
(Teabing, p343)

Please read Using Connect Bible Studies *(page 3) before leading a Bible study with this material.*

Opening Questions

Choose one of these questions.

Is the church trusted generally in this country? Why/why not?	Are you more likely to trust religious leaders or be suspicious? Why?
What do you think of the way Brown portrays the Roman Catholic church?	Had you heard of Opus Dei before you read *The Da Vinci Code*? What is your reaction to Brown's portrayal of it?

Summary

While Robert and Sophie are busy escaping from the police and deciphering codes, the murdering monk Silas is obeying the directions of the mysterious Teacher to get to the keystone before they do. The keystone will purportedly lead them to the Holy Grail, and the truth about the origins of Christianity. For the Teacher, this is not only a lifelong quest, but also lucrative. He has enticed Bishop Aringarosa of Opus Dei to join him in the search, but is charging him 20 million euros. The Bishop obtains the money from the Vatican ostensibly as a separation payment for Opus Dei. The latter is threatened with expulsion from Roman Catholicism because of dubious enrolment practices and their support of corporal mortification, in which members punish themselves physically for sin.

Meanwhile, Teabing tells Robert and Sophie that the Roman Catholic Church deliberately suppressed the truth about Christian history. The Knights Templar discovered documents about Mary Magdalene when they were based in Jerusalem in the twelfth century AD. The church was supposed to be venerating the sacred feminine represented by Mary, not worshipping Jesus as God, and Jesus did not rise from the dead. The Gospels, the doctrine of Jesus' divinity, were all doctored by the Emperor Constantine in the third century, mainly for political ends. Ever since, the Vatican had been complicit in keeping their dubious origins quiet. In addition it had demonised the feminine, conducted witch hunts, and generally suppressed women. Teabing encourages Robert and Sophie in their search, eager that the truth be told and that the church be exposed as suppressive and duplicitous.

Key Issue: Religious authorities

Although Brown is careful to exonerate both Opus Dei and the Roman Catholic Church from any involvement in the murders of *The Da Vinci Code*, he still accuses the church of suppressing universal truth. He does not backtrack on his suggestion, through Leigh Teabing, that Christianity is based on a lie. He implies that the church would be only too willing to cover up any threat to its history. His portrayal of church leadership is restricted to men who want to uphold their own positions of power. So we ask in this study what the Bible thinks of those with leadership responsibilities. What does it say about those who suppress truth, abuse their positions or who play power games?

Chapters to read:

Read chapters 54 to 81.

Bible Study

Choose one question from each section.

1   Leadership – abuse of authority

> *'...if the Church finds the Holy Grail, they will destroy it. The documents and the relics of the blessed Mary Magdalene as well ... all evidence will be lost. The Church will have won their age-old war to rewrite history.'* (Teabing, p358)

◆   Read 1 Samuel 2:12–17,22–36. In what ways were Eli and his sons abusing their position of leadership? How did God – and Eli – view this?

◆   Read John 5:1–23. How was Jesus bringing truth? Who was trying to 'suppress' him and why?

2 Leadership – power struggles?

> *If all went as planned tonight in Paris, Aringarosa would soon be in possession of something that would make him the most powerful man in Christendom.*
> (p150)

◆ Read 1 Kings 18:16–40. What was at stake here? Compare the behaviour of Elijah and the prophets of Baal.

Leaders: Israel was in the grip of a severe drought. King Ahab had a reputation for ignoring God, while his wife Jezebel murdered God's prophets, and encouraged Baal worship. Worship of Baal, the Canaanite god of fertility and strength, and of Ashtoreth his consort, goddess of war and fertility, involved sacred prostitution and sometimes child sacrifice. The behaviour of the prophets of Baal was presumably their usual ritualistic style.

◆ Read Acts 8:9–25. Describe Simon's character and desires. What was the clash in this story really about?

3 Leadership – in print?

> *'The Sangreal documents simply tell the other side of the Christ story. In the end, which side of the story you believe becomes a matter of faith and personal exploration, but at least the information has survived.'* (Teabing, p343)

◆ Read 2 Kings 22:1 – 23:7. What effects did the discovery have and why? Why was God lenient with Josiah?

Leaders: Scholarly opinion is divided over whether this book was a copy of the first five books of the Old Testament, or some or all of Deuteronomy.

◆ Read 2 Peter 1:1 – 2:3. What is Peter wanting to encourage in his readers? How does he define the basis for his confidence?

4 Leadership – the real thing

> *'Silas … if you have learned nothing from me, please … learn this … forgiveness is God's greatest gift … Silas, you must pray.'* (p547)

◆ Read 1 Kings 3:1–15,29–34. In what ways did Solomon's reign have a great beginning? What was he appreciated for?

◆ Read 1 Timothy 1:1–20. How does Paul advise Timothy to exercise his authority? What truth is he eager to celebrate?

Implications

'My dear, the Church has two thousand years of experience pressuring those who threaten to unveil its lies. Since the days of Constantine, the Church has successfully hidden the truth about Mary Magdalene and Jesus.' (Teabing, p534)

Choose one or more of the following questions.

◆ Have you, or someone you know, suffered from abuse by church leaders? Are there issues which should be dealt with?

◆ What would you say to someone who suspects that Brown may be right, and that the church has suppressed historical truth about Jesus and Mary Magdalene?

◆ Do you see power struggles in your church? Why do you think they happen, and is there anything you can do to improve the situation?

◆ What are the qualities of good leadership, and how can you encourage them in yourself and in others?

◆ Why do you think Jesus still attracts so much opposition?

◆ What is the difference between blind unquestioning faith in leaders, and supportive trust of them?

◆ How can we be trustworthy as church members, as far as the wider public is concerned?

◆ How responsible are you with Christian truth as you understand it? Does it have implications for your life which you ignore? How can you change this?

Prayer

Spend some time praying through these issues.

Members' Sheet – *The Da Vinci Code* Part 3

Summary

While Robert and Sophie are busy escaping from the police and deciphering codes, the murdering monk Silas is obeying the directions of the mysterious Teacher to get to the keystone before they do. The keystone will purportedly lead them to the Holy Grail, and the truth about the origins of Christianity. For the Teacher, this is not only a lifelong quest, but also lucrative. He has enticed Bishop Aringarosa of Opus Dei to join him in the search, . but is charging him 20 million euros. The Bishop obtains the money from the Vatican ostensibly as a separation payment for Opus Dei. The latter is threatened with expulsion from Roman Catholicism because of dubious enrolment practices and their support of corporal mortification, in which members punish themselves physically for sin.

Meanwhile, Teabing tells Robert and Sophie that the Roman Catholic Church deliberately suppressed the truth about Christian history. The Knights Templar discovered documents about Mary Magdalene when they were based in Jerusalem in the twelfth century AD. The church was supposed to be venerating the sacred feminine represented by Mary, not worshipping Jesus as God, and Jesus did not rise from the dead. The Gospels, the doctrine of Jesus' divinity, were all doctored by the Emperor Constantine in the third century, mainly for political ends. Ever since, the Vatican had been complicit in keeping their dubious origins quiet. In addition it had demonised the feminine, conducted witch hunts, and generally suppressed women. Teabing encourages Robert and Sophie in their search, eager that the truth be told and that the church be exposed as suppressive and duplicitous.

Key Issue

Bible Study notes

Implications

Prayer

www.connectbiblestudies.com

connect

linking the Word to the world

The Da Vinci Code

Dan Brown (Corgi, 2003)

Part 4: Authentic faith

'Almost everything our fathers taught about Christ is **false.***'*
(Teabing, p318)

Please read Using Connect Bible Studies *(page 3) before leading a Bible study with this material.*

Opening Questions

Choose one of these questions.

What questions would you ask Silas and Bishop Aringarosa about their faith, if you could?	Is there any genuine faith in *The Da Vinci Code*?
Does everyone have a faith? Why/why not?	What is faith?

Summary

While Robert and Sophie seem agnostic about the Christian faith at the beginning of the story, Silas is introduced as a devoted member of the Roman Catholic group Opus Dei, complete with leg-pinching cilice belt for self-punishment. His violent past means that he does not question too deeply the things the Teacher asks him to do in the name of his faith, which include murdering the four leaders of Sion.

Bishop Aringarosa, Silas' friend and mentor, is consumed by his passion to save Opus Dei from excommunication, to the extent of trusting the Teacher who turns out to be a murderer himself.

Silas dies violently, while the Bishop recovers in hospital from the shootout with the police. He and the devout Catholic Captain Fache are both repentant of their mixed motives in the affair. Aringarosa had assured Silas that God is a God who forgives.

Robert and Sophie are drawn into the chase for the truth as explained by Teabing. The cunning knight is using them to get to the keystone, but insists true faith is older than Christianity – it is veneration of the sacred feminine which needs to be restored to its rightful place by exposing the Holy Grail to the world. However, Robert and Sophie are horrified to discover that Teabing is the instigator behind Saunière's murder, and also those of his manservant and the other Sion leaders. Teabing is the Teacher.

The police catch up with Teabing as Robert refuses to tell him what the final code means. Sophie discovers she is a descendant of Mary Magdalene and is reunited with a grandmother and brother she did not know she had. But the whereabouts of the Holy Grail – documents detailing the truth about Jesus' lineage, and Mary's bones – remain a mystery. Unless of course, they are resting beneath the double pyramid at the Louvre…

Key Issue: Authentic faith

Silas puts his faith in Bishop Aringarosa and Opus Dei; the Bishop trusts the Teacher; the Vatican seems to trust nobody; Saunière trusts Sophie to discover his secret; Robert and Sophie put their faith in each other. There's lots of faith then, inside the world of *The Da Vinci Code*. Outside its world however, the book has caused many to ask questions of faith itself. While Christians respond with varying degrees of hostility or fascination to *The Da Vinci Code*, we finish our study by asking again the big questions of Christianity. Do we need to punish ourselves for our sins, as Silas believed? Did Jesus rise from the dead, rather than commit his church to Mary? Why was he crucified? Was he/is he the Son of God?

Chapters to read:

Read chapters 82 to the Epilogue.

Bible Study

Choose one question from each section.

1   Faith in self-inflicted painful penance?

> **I must purge my soul of today's sins. *The sins committed today had been holy in purpose … Forgiveness was assured. Even so, Silas knew, absolution required sacrifice … Exhaling slowly, he savoured the cleansing ritual of his pain.*** (p29)

◆ Read Leviticus 16:1–34. Why does God take sin so seriously? What does solving the problem involve?

◆ Read Philippians 3:1 – 4:1. Where did Paul's confidence come from? What part do Paul's own efforts play?

2   Faith in the son of God

> *'Right,' Teabing said. 'Jesus' establishment as "the Son of God" was officially proposed and voted on by the Council of Nicaea.'*
> *'Hold on. You're saying Jesus' divinity was the result of a vote?'* (p315)

You may like to follow the passage from John through to the next question.

◆   Read Matthew 11:1–29. What reactions did Jesus provoke in others? What did Jesus say about faith in himself?

◆   Read John 1:1–50. How does the writer define who Jesus is? In what way did others respond to Jesus?

3   Faith in Jesus' mission

> *'But you told me the New Testament is based on fabrications.'*
> *Langdon smiled. 'Sophie, every faith in the world is based on fabrication. That is the definition of faith – acceptance of that which we imagine to be true, that which we cannot prove.'* (p451)

◆   Read Isaiah 53:1–12. Describe the person Isaiah is prophesying about. How does this passage inspire faith?

◆   Read John 1:1–50. How does the writer describe what Jesus came to do? What was John the Baptist's role?

4   Faith in the resurrection

> *'What happens … if persuasive scientific evidence comes out that the Church's version of the Christ story is inaccurate, and that the greatest story ever told is, in fact, the greatest story ever sold?'* (Teabing, p356)

◆   Read John 20:19–31. What differences did and does the presence of Jesus make?

◆   Read Luke 24:13–35. What happened to the hopes of the two walkers? What was the impact of Jesus being unrecognisable at first?

Implications

A very wise British priest noted in the press recently, 'Christian theology has survived the writings of Galileo and the writings of Darwin. Surely it will survive the writings of some novelist from New Hampshire.' (Dan Brown, www.danbrown.com/media)

Choose one or more of the following questions.

- What would you say to someone who thinks that Jesus was just a good man, and that the suggestions of *The Da Vinci Code* are entirely feasible?

- Are there ways in which you punish yourself for perceived wrong behaviour? How could you change this?

- Why do we need a saviour today?

- What would you say to Dan Brown, if you got the chance? Why?

- Are there areas of your faith that have been shaken by *The Da Vinci Code*? Do you need to talk these through with your group?

- Some church leaders say that Jesus did not need to rise from the dead in a literal, bodily form for Christianity to be true. How would you answer this?

- Do you need to take your own 'road to Emmaus' and search out the facts and history behind your faith?

- What is your experience of the risen Jesus? How does it affect your response to something like *The Da Vinci Code*?

Prayer

Spend some time praying through these issues.

Members' Sheet – *The Da Vinci Code* Part 4

Summary

While Robert and Sophie seem agnostic about the Christian faith at the beginning of the story, Silas is introduced as a devoted member of the Roman Catholic group Opus Dei, complete with leg-pinching cilice belt for self-punishment. His violent past means that he does not question too deeply the things the Teacher asks him to do in the name of his faith, which include murdering the four leaders of Sion.

Bishop Aringarosa, Silas' friend and mentor, is consumed by his passion to save Opus Dei from excommunication, to the extent of trusting the Teacher who turns out to be a murderer himself. Silas dies violently, while the Bishop recovers in hospital from the shootout with the police. He and the devout Catholic Captain Fache are both repentant of their mixed motives in the affair. Aringarosa had assured Silas that God is a God who forgives.

Robert and Sophie are drawn into the chase for the truth as explained by Teabing. The cunning knight is using them to get to the keystone, but insists true faith is older than Christianity – it is veneration of the sacred feminine which needs to be restored to its rightful place by exposing the Holy Grail to the world. However, Robert and Sophie are horrified to discover that Teabing is the instigator behind Saunière's murder, and also those of his manservant and the other Sion leaders. Teabing is the Teacher.

The police catch up with Teabing as Robert refuses to tell him what the final code means. Sophie discovers she is a descendant of Mary Magdalene and is reunited with a grandmother and brother she did not know she had. But the whereabouts of the Holy Grail – documents detailing the truth about Jesus' lineage, and Mary's bones – remain a mystery. Unless of course, they are resting beneath the double pyramid at the Louvre...

Key Issue

Bible Study notes

Implications

Prayer